The Right Place to Jump

Peter Covino

New Issues Poetry & Prose

A Green Rose Book

New Issues Poetry & Prose
The College of Arts and Sciences
Western Michigan University
Kalamazoo, Michigan 49008

First Edition, 2012.

ISBN: 978-1-936970-09-4 (paperbound)

Library of Congress Cataloging-in-Publication Data:
Covino, Peter.
The Right Place to Jump/Peter Covino
Library of Congress Control Number: 2011943424

Editor:	William Olsen
Guest Editor:	Nancy Eimers
Managing Editor:	Kimberly Kolbe
Layout Editor:	Elizabyth A. Hiscox
Assitant Editor:	Traci Brimhall
Art Director:	Paul Sizer
Designer:	Scott McManus
Production:	Paul Sizer
	The Design Center, Frostic School of Art
	College of Fine Arts
	Western Michigan University
Printing:	McNaughton & Gunn, Inc.

The Right Place to Jump

Peter Covino

New Issues

WESTERN MICHIGAN UNIVERSITY

The Right Place to Jump

Also by Peter Covino

Cut Off the Ears of Winter
Straight Boyfriend

For Donald Revell

Contents

I.

Sri Lanka 7
Built on the Foundation of What Isn't True 8
The Weight of Water 9
No Jobs at the Fiat Plant 11
Erotics of Longing: Black-Eyed 13
"Her Eyes Flew Open" 15
S. Kensington, January 17
"Such a Drag to Want Something Sometime" 18
The River 21
Eternal Mercy Hallmark Card 25
66 Trees 27
More Than a Verb, a Nation 30
Broken Kingdom 31
An Oyster Leads a Dreadful but Exciting Life... 33
Pliers: A Resolution 35
Theory of Ultimate Willfulness 36
Millennial Wyoming in Unpopular Imagination,
   with Codeine 37

II.

Visit to San Francisco 41
Chelsea Apartments Emptying 42
Home Movies 43
Heroin 45
Dress Rehearsal 46
"Tell It to My Heart" 48
Iowa Landscape 51
Serendi(pity) 53
Bad Trick 56
Bewitched, Bedraggled, December 58
Disappearance and Modulation 59
Earthly Possessions (*Errata*) 61
Mise-en-scène 62
Malevich: Thirty-Four Drawings 64
Montecassino 65
Zion (Two Sketches) 66
Harvest 68
The Grand Central Clock Will Be Tired Again 69
Roma Auto 70
Dear Reader: Questions about Sugar 73
Rain Delay 74

I.

Sri Lanka

Reading Celan:

when the heart swells
can He still speak through us

       inner ruminating
       cornered death knell
            of the other side

spindled-
      heaven in an earthbound
      warning

      *

channeled incorrectly
rubberstamped signs: a red postmark
            a dead bee limb

& tentacles of sun among the many-headed daffodils
water-thick stemmed through a mason jar:
      vinegar-clean missives

      *

don't suppose the blue glass candles
      tropical/hand painted/imported

they're dime store bought
      scent of ocean

constituted objects
      to be returned

      *

last night empty-stomached

I devoured my God
made love, in the name of

      the reverent

Built on the Foundation of What Isn't True

—based on a documentary film about dancer John Henry

That moment scars his back. The folded flag?
In German (the voice-over) on his imaginary way
Back from Vietnam. Almost directionless the sweep
Away from him in the distance. The medics
Who identify the dead lover, over 6'2".

"Of course men were having sex with each other;
We had to bring the pieces of him home
For last rites." Was that the time to tell anybody?
Incontinence—like sugar to a diabetic.

*

Who cares if he's lying: AIDS or war veteran;
Most of the time gender is constructed.
Those regrets: truth and not enough
Fabrications or inconsistencies.

The valiant soldier as metaphor for illness—
Are you in pain? Exquisitely ghosting?

*

                        In that climactic scene
Where he dances the ravages of the body
He's wearing too many clothes.

Where's the hard-on for death? Bone and sinew.
Those early performances gone.
A kind of haunting to hope for.
Photographs and clay. Each time the first time.

The Weight of Water

What of the scraping, the abandonment, the nearly imperceptible
sucking sound that type of mollusk makes as it quickly multiplies,

drains the life out of the lake. Signs everywhere warn
to scrub the bottom of oars, treat the boat with bleach, steel wool.

And what of the reckless scraping—Heidegger might argue
for a wholeness of being, the purity of worldly things, drift and graft

of the motion of water. Incandescent sea life and lake algae,
nonetheless visible in opaque brownness. Your splayed legs,

frivolous enough, then three times the size in the underwater reflection.
On the edge of the dock empty now, an orange chair—sole sentinel

such bright orange, keeping watch. And soon, another summer will pass
with all its loneliness and my closed-lip assurances, you *won't* go blind
    at forty.

What about the fresh water fish? That mad phenomenon called feeding
the lake, to attract tourists: trout-fed streams also nearby, fly-fishing

with locally tied trout flies, no matter the catch has to be thrown
back or else we too will glow from PCBs. This morning our swim

at Cream Hill, the town lake beach, more a pond, the dawn's so still
we hear the plastic garbage can clawed by raccoons in the night.

Can-opener sharp in its edges: everything redeemable. The sun
brightly yellows the pond's surface, euphonious mix of mist and gnats.

How impressive the residue, littered sand, the wrappers; toys
left along the shore and a perfectly folded-over blanket. Earlier

your imprint in the bed as you trudged off to make coffee, the alarm
waking and not waking us. Remarkably, love starts again each day

though I'm having trouble breathing, and you remind me my allergy
medication's probably off. Your words and the smell of you linger.

Such fascination water holds for me, in the hot dry sun. I am thankful
for everything: for the outhouse and farm animals of my youth;

for this daily cycle of forgetfulness; the cool afternoons in the eaves
of the main church, better than a tour guide's visit to San Lorenzo.

Even if the compressor on the air conditioner isn't
quite working right, it's August and we're alive.

No Jobs at the Fiat Plant

The northern savages
To get to them
On foot or donkey

Walk through the valley
Of Grottaminarda
Not the underwater glow

In the distance
The distance from marble
Marbled tongues

Of fable, no jobs
A ship—not steerage
Construction

Never another weapon
Words the worst kind
Shouting

Gravel words
For gargle
Gravel-gargle with hands

A blown horn in fog
Water on metal
A beat-up rental car

No job at the Fiat plant
Snow on the olive trees
Persimmon uncultivated

Now—persimmon in snow
On the trees
Uncultivated, now

Snow on the olive trees
Cries from the mountains
Coffee-bitter sting

Of exhaustion
Glass light
Through trees

Sunday, waking
On the porch
Canisters

Of citronella
Candles
Unlike the grottoes

Not like the flowers
Neither the dehumidifier
Sanction the collar

Wind chime, chirpers
The noise the wings
Make

Erotics of Longing: Black-Eyed

Late August flower—
left crimson reflector, shiner,
baseball cap pulled low:
"get rid of the lover"
I tell the guy at the gym....

No justice, cousin,
how that husband decorated
your floor—shot to
molecular bits
leaving you with two

children, beckoning.
The Science Times, Tuesday,
argues for *spaghettification*
neologism—and what happens
to the soul when it's torn

in bifurcated angst
falling through time's
black hole—as each
piece separates
continuously—

where it can still
clock time but not tell—
to clock, verb, also
as a brick in the mind's
patchwork, blood work,

yellow-suited spacemen
collecting remains,
a show beyond worse
on the dirty-job-someone's-
got-to continuum

midsummer, and we
hadn't seen each other
in ten years, the funeral
parlor heavy
with gladioli

showy chrysanthemum
his depression—I lined
the front flowerbed
with the Latinate
epithet for you,

rudbeckia speciosa,
brokenness,
robber baron—
barren though
determined

"Her Eyes Flew Open"

Between gulps of water and a strange
Insistence the Indian food not be spicy—
She *must* be pregnant—Dr. Sue Park
Nauseous and cautious now
Tells of a recent patient:

A forty-two-year-old perfectly healthy
Cerebral hemorrhage
Who barely
Complained of a headache
Moments earlier and would,

Ethical questions aside,
Immediately need to be coded
Because the patient's next of kin
Is anxious to donate the organs
To science.

Another anesthesiologist friend
Suspects a conspiracy and rails
About the usual evils
Of Western capitalism
The corruption

Of the overpriced transplant business,
How doctors are pressured
To remove all usable organs and keep
Them fresh as possible.
As I'm trying unsuccessfully

To get someone to pass
The tandoori lamb;
Desperate now
For some curried something
Or naan, at least, anything

To soothe my *own* queasy stomach
As the waiter brings
A decanted magnum of *Barbera d'Alba*
And tells us to be sure to drink
The wine slowly because...

It's still breathing,
In shock
From being opened....
Then our friend describes
How afterward the heart

Needs to be restarted
Vessels cauterized
So the transplant doctors can make
A clean incision, preserve
Motor function.

On this eve of her first sonogram,
Dr. Park adds, "Well,
Though the woman will
Never be able to talk or walk
Perhaps she could still feel.

And we felt devastated
For coding her so soon;
We would have preferred
To wait a week,
But without a will or health proxy

The transplant team arrived
Exactly five minutes after
She flatlined.
When they cut into her,
Her face twitched

And her eyes
Flew open,
A customary reflex
We'd read and heard about
But never experienced firsthand."

S. Kensington, January

Battersea (nature):

Red-beaked cloughs, two, in a room-size cage,

Perched on a Japanese green point pine (and later a pagoda),

Distressed green, darker hunter

In the one hour of sunshine so far this month

Across the candied Prince Albert Bridge, pink Beaux Arts port holes

All night the ring-necks shrieking, red-and-yellow billed

A parrot too that jumps stealthily and often from wet tree

Limb to fence side...low clouds moving west in a painting

Of clouds....

Natural History Museum (nature morte):

A mighty fortress

Is my God all night cloughs chirping; the afternoon our reflection

In formalin-filled glass cases—faded by water and light

Through rows and floors of non-passerine depredation, peering—

Buteo ventralis 1837, the larger angular *phalcoboenus*,

Forty-six contained inches of wingspan, Santa Cruz, Patagonia, April 1st.

As far back as the *H.M.S. Beagle*, the red trail

Around the Southern hemisphere.

"Such a Drag to Want Something Sometime"

...one thing leads to another, I know
—Chrissie Hynde

Halloween, 1984 and I'm dressed-up as the Pretenders,
    the whole early-80s punk rock group,
        all four of them, at Chi Psi's Drink-

A-Thong costume party in this clichéd LL Bean
    catalog liberal arts college. I'm just back
        from a summer backpacking

through Europe where I've discovered Gucci,
    Sun-In, and bisexuality with a vengeance.
        With this newly-affected

Euro-trash accent, I'm determined to sleep with anyone
    who's breathing: the ticket-collector
        at a favorite art house movie theatre;

the dishwasher at Hot Wok's Chinese Restaurant;
    the junior faculty, especially that Anthropology prof.
        who accidentally singed

the sheepish bulimic girl's hair. There's Steve ---------,
    Greek American captain of my captain,
        on the lacrosse team

whose glistening, towel-clad mid-section always seemed
    to be at eye-level and a quick change away.
        I'm sporting a Flock of Seagulls flip

six inches across the front of my face, beneath two wigs,
    and thick black eyeliner. "The Adultress"
        and "Bad Boys Get Spanked"

are the panacea for this testosterone-fueled androgynous
    angst. I'm 80s updated-psychedelia personified.
        A computer generated 3-D hologram

in the days of erasable typewriter paper. In 1982, at the height
        of their fame, lead guitarist, James Honeyman Scott's
                speedballed heart implodes.

Less than a year later, bassist Pete Farndon's found
        channel swimming, drowned in his own bathtub.
                Maybe the Internet could have saved them,

some Narcotics Anonymous web site or good porn
        on hump week nights. In spite of the bright lights
                decade of dead disco and stifled activism,

even moperockers crave the occasional oblivious fun.
        One of Martin Chambers' actual drum sticks
                is looped to my belt, his blown-up

visage pinned to my chest. In one hand I'm clutching
        Farndon's papier-mâché head strangled by his works,
                with the needle still attached

as I maneuver toward the staggering footballers—
        wasted on Jagermeister and heteronormativity,
                and every bit as horrifying.

My girlfriend, at the time, let's call her Fran, sad woman,
        has promised to dress as a dominatrix and walk
                me around in a harness and leash.

But she's a stoned no show and the damn leash catches
        on everything: once on a door handle
                that almost choked me.

Another time on Rob Bradhurst, star defensive end,
        who pulled so close we almost kissed. My bob-
                length wigs swivel on command:

Chrissie Hynde on the scraggly pitch-black side, borrowed
        Stratocaster slung crotch low and Honeyman Scott
                on the bleach blond side

left nostril flared open, trailing fake blood. *Is it time*
   to stop the sobbing, yet? I ended up passed out
     in some spoiled New York City

trust funder's posh dorm room. Our lipstick and
   makeup smeared; our necks stiff from all
     the soothe-less tangle.

Not such a far cry from these recent nights
   of thwarted hook-ups—in some
     expensive chat room—

when suddenly the sun starts to brighten the skies,
   and, in a couple of hours, I still
     gotta get up for work.

The River

In the dream of the river, the sound of water
Rushing, water roaring: sounds
Like animal sounds, human sounds, both:
You have loved me too well and not enough....

I can't smell the water in spite of its murkiness—
Curious, since I'm so close I can see mud
Moving over water, water over mud.

    Whenever he wanted, he'd beat her,
    Because dinner was late;
    She cooked him rice again.

    He especially hates rice, reminds him of the war.
    Paltry meals where Ingrid visited his bunk,
    Slinking past S.S. guards, promising favors
    In lavender negligees, embroidered slippers—

    Just to sneak him sugar—so the rice tasted like sweet ricotta.

In the fourth dream, chemotherapy:
A cancer patient, a client from work,
The smell physically lingers:
I can't clear it from memory

    ...it was as if the shame of it must outlive him—Kafka

    To clean him you say? Use warm water.
    Because he's uncircumcised.
    & *how* did you punish yourself afterward?
    Afterward.

In the field where I'm running, being chased
Tiring, I can't bring myself to stop,
I can't decipher my surroundings clearly.

    My running is a film with alternating backgrounds.

In the dream of the reclining woman,
Her voice forms slowly out of the darkness of air.
She's lying beside me not protesting my advances.
This absence of protest startles me.

When I dress in drag
He thinks I'm my sister
I like flirting; I don't feel so bad.

In the first dream I'm on a playing field,
Running, running
& being chased
By someone I don't know.

The field is vaguely familiar, slopes
Upward from tennis courts
That haven't been used in a while.
The field is moist.

My feet slip, my body becomes heavy.

You hate yourself?
You don't hate yourself.
You work hard to support a family.

On the field where the dreams begin
To intersect, I'm struggling, running
Harder, battling the inevitable convergence
Of rivers, bodies of water seek each other out.

Water, yes, water is allowed.

I'll think I'm my sister,
When I dress in drag.
It won't hurt me much....

In bed with the woman,
I admire her lush, full body,
not unlike a Veronese painting
& just as lifelike or unlifelike.

The woman whispers to me
From a blank space
Where our mouths should be.
She's telling me something urgent,

An insistent hush.
Her voice & the invitation of her body
Dissonant.

I am not running away from anyone
I'm trying to outrun an opponent as in a race,
Though I don't know
Who the opponent is.

       I'll be a flirt; I'll let him touch me
       But not call me names.

       The river frightens me also.

In the drowned river my youngest sister calls to me
For help and the river is louder now.
I can hear it, feel the rush
& I can hear my sister calling out my name—

       My mother sometimes fought back,
       But she'd bruise easily
       & lie to her Chinese co-workers
       At the dress shop;

As a threat, you don't eat.
You say you know *how* to suffer.
To cleanse yourself,
You don't bathe?

       They ate rice every day
       In delicate bone-china bowls,
       Rice with Chinese vegetables,
       Water-chestnuts, Chinese spinach, snap-peas.

The cancer patient, from work,
Talked non-stop about death today
& the woman in bed asks me
To hold her tighter. But I don't

Because this closeness
Will drown us,
Although we're not in the river and my sister *is* in the river,

Becoming more distant, spiraling out of sight.

Eternal Mercy Hallmark Card

He spanned the straight
years; last link
to the almost wife
& then my parents' three-year

silence. Dr. Bjordahl
supremely patient—
slobbering fool I was
barely able to see

the euthanasia line,
the toll-free numbers
for pet-grief counseling—
can you believe there's

such a thing? Friday.
End of the week lull.
A scotch. Then
the last sedative

for Sweetie. Please
don't put my cat
in a plastic bag.
(I can't bear it.)

Not the plastic
we wrap the Southern
plants in, the fig tree
plastic.... So I phoned

my mother who offered
to speak to the doctor
although she doesn't
speak English—

"just leave him in
the carrying case!"
The Delta pet carrier,
which I did

and Dr. Bjordahl
promised to wrap
him in a towel
to keep him

in the icebox,
until the cremation man
picked him up,
sometime the next week.

66 Trees

of course I wish him dead
abusively inside me
I think of him in parts

as in that devastating Fassbinder movie
starring his Moroccan lover—both of whom
had terrible truncated ends

Yesterday morning in a bleary-eyed
anxious preflight return-to-my-east-coast-life
I learned L's still in a coma at a rehab center in Queens

she showed signs of visual tracking, twice
close to a miracle, and squeezed her husband's hand

*

66 trees because we counted them

and took pictures for the police report

cut down in the backyard, the thickness
like so many body bags, bone bright white birch,
among the graying drizzled upper field

stone walls more visible
the neighbor's house, view, and market value improved

*

we must be reading the same books
that monograph on Proust,
and the anecdote about the rats in the male brothel
a twisted metaphor for identity and gratification
understandable given the era

therefore thicker, older
and we priced trees that weekend
in persistent rain
in the mist air sprays that work to keep them alive

a growing copper beech, twelve inches in diameter
costs $10,000, once you see the silvery-coppery
gnarled bark there's no forgetting, no mistaking

*

believe me with L's health and another suicide—
I'm left with a huge hole and writing
seems worthless, $1,100 worth
of vandalism and a car rental later

who can focus on this yoga bullshit

enough for a psychic breakdown
everything's come to a ground-down halt
difficult to fathom: another handsome gay man
drowned in faraway Puerto Rico—
emblematic... & meanwhile

I have pantry moths and a strained check book...

in another email her toddler's locked
in the bathroom playing with the toilet plunger

what are pantry moths anyway?

*

Today, all day, at my mother's house she interrupted me
while I was working, because I don't see her enough
and she's getting older, the ways older gets—

what I'm afraid is falsely recovered
66 trees, body bags

the insides of the bags,
stuck inside the unfolded plastic

smoldering-mulching trees
what I'm afraid of

the missed-numbed decade
the ruthless fugue state I grapple
trucked down trunked down
bitter crop

*

as I read—by the *only* gay Italian poet
who died of AIDS in 1996—*Il poeta assassinato*,
another book on the subject of Pier Paolo Pasolini
and his murder by a gang of gay pickups

intense days, thinking about eighteen-year-old prostitutes
and the career-making obit of a dear poet-suicide
there's a (w)hole (world) through the back window of my car
and I probably need a new boyfriend

More Than a Verb, a Nation

Vetted he's always saying
Should I imagine Uncle Sam horned purple
By war conspicuous in the 1966 edition
'cept for Texas
Where I know I know we got our own ranch
I'm trying not to pick on where you left off
Where the perfect makeup or the dusty
Mauve wrap entitled you to miss my class
@ $2,500 per semester, without insurance

But I'm ill-equipped to complain
A dictum's gotta be more than one-dimensional
So I arc the vetted V.
& wed past & tense to the gerund
For a star clustering constellation
5:40 a.m. in that fluorescent before saying

I can be heavy-lidded or drawing on the board

Belatedly and not enough

Dear M.
Meant to say hi
Other night
But I get shy
And beaten down

I'm having trouble with agreement and good verbs.
I waited for the water filter to filter.
I ordered 30 gifts from the Home Shopping Channel and sent 29 back.

Broken Kingdom

Always check expiration dates.
& indulge a mother's fear the eggplant's
Overcooked/oversalted but still excellent.

Be sure to lock the storage closet door
From the wrong side out like that Cary Grant movie
Where he moves to the Connecticut suburbs.

Must everything be metaphor? The bishop's
Gaudy miter from the Easter service where light
Shone through the resurrection window on cue?

You wonder about a new coffeemaker,
& why all the daffodils on the coffee table
But one is dead. You cut the tip off

To let that one bloom. 78° in March—
Winter to summer in a day &
It feels so odd to open the window

After weeks of rain. Everything: the red-tailed
Hawk perched on the telephone line during
A conversation with your best friend, a car salesman

As you warily change the date
Of the said act, since you both had a sighting
Of the Virgin. Even though said sighting

Was before said act, you don't want to alarm anyone.
For your most trusted confidantes & the therapist
Some semblance of truth

Casually stated to hide the real fear
Two months before a wedding (of sorts)
With another person, conveniently, a man

Whom of course you never tell
& lie to.
Always check expiration dates.

Though rationally it only lasted
A few seconds, three thrusts
At most until you noticed

Through the grape latex—part of you
So lovingly, desiringly
Amidst implied action

Which led to said act
And all this inconvenient
Misdirected panic.

An Oyster Leads a Dreadful but Exciting Life...

Reading MFK Fisher

She may spawn several hundred million eggs, fifteen to one hundred
    million at a time.
It is hoped, sentimentally at least, that the spat—our spat—enjoys
    himself.
He devotes himself to drinking:
He can easily handle twenty-six or -seven quarts an hour.
Then one day, maternal longings surge between his two valves
And he becomes a she!

Cupidinous.

Danger lurks everywhere: duck-slipper-mussel-Black-Drum-leech
    sponge-borer and
The hated starfish. (Men try to catch it with things called star-mops.)
Life is hard, we say. An oyster's worse:

Oyster Stew

----

1 quart oyster	*4 tablespoons butter*
2 cups oyster liquor	*celery salt*
2 cups heavy cream	*pepper*

*Bring 1 cup of oyster liquor to a boil and when it has cooked
for 5 minutes skim off the top. Cook the oysters in a cup of
liquor until the edges curl. Add cream, butter and seasoning
to taste, etc.*

----

*Celery salt in this recipe can almost be called "New England"
    now.

Fear not:
The unpleasant truth of a bad oyster is that it would immediately
    taste
Thoroughly nasty, though men's ideas continue to run in the old
    channels about oysters
As well as God, war, and women—

Naked
Cracked open in the shells
In the cool fresh grayness of dawn

Cicero ate them to nourish his eloquence.
They prevent goiter.
Somewhere after 1461 Louis XI made them obligatory.
In the times of Voltaire, Pope, and Swift they were considered
    aperitifs.

Huitres en Couquilles à la Rockerfeller
(An endearing bit of chichi)
Tonier than any Louisiana oyster bar.

Heating them can make them infamous.

Never iced

Their omission:
A sure sign of internal disintegration, as if Ma came to church in
    her corset-cover
Or Uncle Jim brought his light-o-love to the children's picnic.

Pliers: A Resolution

Space between trees
& a zipper:

Children's laughter
What's inside? Opens up

Playing in the next room

Rhubarb's bounce
In the mouth

On the plains
O Nebraska

With strawberries
Beneath the fence—

Keep the rabbits out
Fennel's rare in these parts

The titmice multiplying

Go on, have a field day

Theory of Ultimate Willfulness

When we walked out to plant
More rain in the words
We noticed the echinacea keeled
Over, top heavy—how much sun
On the rocks today! where a lizard
Skitters back into the foundation,
Into this etymology of planting
Two thick inches of mulch
Even as the wisteria thrives
Threatening to blossom
Long after its season
And the clematis takes hold
Climbing as it does toward the heaven
Of our screened-in porch.

Millennial Wyoming in Unpopular Imagination, with Codeine

Until that day after minor surgery, he believed
most of Wyoming was a factory specializing
in night-lights and bars of soap decorated with
images of bucking broncos or upright prairie dogs.

Until that anesthetic morning at Salt Lake University
Hospital where all the afflicted of the Mountain West
congregate—the only research hospital for miles—
he'd never met a real live person from Wyoming.

Eugene, his suite-mate, originally from Oregon
strangely enough, was a curious combination
of vanity and American fanatical. His voice
raspy as tumbleweed and his face,

from years of born-again vitriol, round
and vivid as a fairground air balloon.
Eugene was rehabbing comfortably from hair
transplant surgery, but in that confused state

he saw a pounding gavel where a heart
should be. He saw a row of bedpans stretched
alongside a highway with signs for Laramie
and Evanston, where you can buy chicken fried

steak, and X-rated paraphernalia. For hours
more and more Wyomians came into the room
with their Chihuahuas and enthusiastic mothers-in-law.
They wanted to set the record straight right there

in the soul of Zion, for all the sins committed against
the scarecrow man, even as the defendants give
more television interviews blowing their pitiful
methamphetamine smoke into the lungs of a new century.

II.

Visit to San Francisco

Like the story of the blind man
who's granted three wishes
yet asks for everything but his sight.

This morning the bells of St. Francis
compete with the caws of gulls
and the rumble and whistle of traffic.

I'm trying not to hate myself—
last night at the Eros, $15 worth
of flesh and unreliable fantasy.

Fueled by a six-pack and the almostness
of an underage conservatory student,
I've ended up, here, as the night before,

wanting titillation, something close to milk
and love, but easier and anonymous—
the surge and response, a blanketing steam.

Sometimes it's the conversation,
scavenge of remains, or the obligatory
questions about positions and ethnicity.

I have traded the burnt tobacco fields
and oleander, the well-illumined necropolis
at the edge of my city, for these ten minutes

of stooped-over bliss. Outside, even
the sidewalks warn of the *continuing wrath*
of the four-lettered devil.

But I seem to have lost my underwear,
my car keys, can't remember the ride back
to the hotel, the alarm, the flight home.

Chelsea Apartments Emptying

for Tory Dent

In Chelsea, apartments are emptying
A market glut, the high price
Of flowers, a squall of doves;
It's monsoon weather.

It's raining in Chelsea
And the high-priced doves
Glut the skies, a monsoon
Of flowers floods the market.

There are empty apartments in Chelsea
And flowers are more expensive
Than doves at the market,
A squall of real estate brokers
Shopping for the highest prices.

She was a dove, above
The monsoon, after the flood,
Before the high prices of apartments
Exceeded the market value,
Just in time.

I'd sell my apartment,
And fight the squalls just to fly
With her
If only I knew how
To stop all this hemorrhaging.

Home Movies

This is a story about two men
who love each other, two men
who meet at a truck stop
in East Texas, twenty-five years ago
and make love on the first date
in the back of a pickup truck.

This is the story of one of those men
driving his pickup truck
to the airport to board a flight
for Florida, to visit the other man,
some years later. This is the story
of the love these two men still
have for each other. One man's
name is John, he lives in Florida,
and the other man's name is Len.

Len still loves John and this visit
happens just before the big hurricane.
Len's rented a camcorder.
Len wants to record this visit.
This is Len's visit before his surgery,
before the hurricane. John pretends
he doesn't want to be recorded, but he does.

In this recording, Len imitates John's dog.
The dog's name is Chaos. Chaos, the dog,
John and Len are all being recorded.
They are being recorded with a camcorder,
before the hurricane. Len is recording
John and then John records Len.
Len records John taking a bath,
Len records Len in the mirror
recording John taking a bath.
Len records John playing his records,
John playing with Chaos.

John records Len playing with Chaos.
Len is shirtless playing with Chaos
and some kind of sick pleasure
comes out of all this recording,
caressing Len with weary lens
in a seductive attempt to take him
back all those years when we thought
it was okay to fuck in a pickup truck
on the first date. John doesn't
want Len to have surgery, he loves Len
just the way he is, the way he was.

John is still recording,
because he wants to preserve everything
just the way it was; John
has asked Len to drive to the airport so John
can continue recording him.
Len does as John asks,
because after all those years
and not much real love in between,
Len feels the least he can do
is everything John asks.

John is recording Len driving
his pickup truck, just before the hurricane's
scheduled to hit. Len's in a hurry
to catch a flight back to Texas again
before the hurricane. Len is driving fast
and crying while John is recording him,
just before the hurricane hits. Len is driving
and crying, before flying home. John isn't
crying. Chaos is in the back of the pickup truck
barking. Len is crying and John isn't crying.
Chaos is getting excited, he's sitting up
in the back of the pickup, barking
and won't stop anytime soon.

Heroin

Last night the snow filled up your arms

tracks of snow from East 2nd Street &

I couldn't dig out your Porsche replace

the curtains in ample free time

paint the changes of the window in the light

little of nothing to hold on to

how the skin peels away *the bugs*

come apart with mayonnaise & honey

Dress Rehearsal

Media: For the manual labor on the man-of-war
The lieutenant with the perpetual toothpick—
For the messages sent to the massage parlors
Of Chicago—the convenience store of crack fixes:
First Gunner, M. Conroy of Muncie, IN
Does hereby bequeath lighter fluid
And more pens, Internet disconnections
To beheadings, canned food and sand-flecked
Whiskers. To the disappearing recruitment
Agent more sleepless nights.

Epitaphs:

The ship of his
Breathing, lapidary

Iron machine holsters
Sans machines; electric air

Maine's plethora of
Beaver remediators,
The non-pornographic
Variety better
For preserving
Landscape

A rhapsody of birds
Above a cemetery road
Or avenue named
For Popes—Sixtus's
Obelisk—a full service
For words more
Conversation than the
Club car

More integral than
Wildly

Intellectually then
Filling

Lecture and bicycle pump
Pi: turn-up the exponential rout
A nip, Rip, a pinup, a pip

"Tell It to My Heart"

Why would Taylor Dayne—D-A-Y-N-E—
be standing outside Penn Station,
& why would she need bodyguards anymore,
dumb ass?
              She of the famous Barry White
cover song and the soul-inflected, freestyle
groove—pop diva of, what was it, the late
80s, early 90s? Bona fide crossover star,
another white girl to appropriate black
musical phrasing: *saying goodbye is never
an easy thing....*

For two weeks now, the same love songs
in my head, forecasting a breakup—
this impending move to another state and only
Taylor understands—straight out of Freeport,
Long Island via years of the demanding
Brighton Beach nightclub scene.

She was standing *this* close to me
& thanked me for recognizing her,
right in front of Penn Station
with two bodyguards on a Tuesday,
2:45 in the afternoon.

Could have been an honest case
of mistaken identity like my friend Richard
who looks uncannily like Kevin Spacey....

Well, at least I think it was her,
4'11" bundle of nerve in heels and
hand-stitched jeans. Maybe it was spring
fever, and nostalgia, or the way the girl
with the barky Shih Tzu made me crazy
by droning on, on her cell phone
about bungee jumping & needing
another cup of coffee.

Maybe she decided not to burst
my bubble, to go along with the happy
coincidence, me her number one fan, after all,
who's belted out many a version
of "Tell it to My Heart"—*tell me*
I'm the only one, after a couple of martinis
at the local karaoke bar.

　　　　　　If it's true
that God paints some people and with others
he forgets the paintbrush altogether—
well, I'll tell you, Taylor's his masterpiece,
pronounced features and all, a natural beauty;
and who cares if she plays second-rate
clubs now like Mohegan Sun and
the Suncoast Casino in Vegas.

　　　　　　I admit it,
I thought she was black too, until recently
when I saw her on the *MTV Jewish
Suburban Legends Special.* For only $9.95
on her web site, you can download three
of her most famous songs and even get
a voiced-over complimentary dedication—
provided you got decent credit.

　　　　　　You were barely
in grammar school, Britney Spears! not even
a Mickey Mouse clubber yet, in 1989,
when Taylor's megahit ballad "Love Will
Lead You Back" *to my arms, I know my love
will lead you back* topped the charts
for a steady six weeks, just in time
for the summer wedding rush.

Can't you just hear it now, that misty,
languid electric piano, the wispy drumbeats,
rhythmic cymbal: quintessential lounge music....

And who can say, after all that spandex and
dreadful news of the 1980s, how many
slow, jubilant dances I danced at Italian
weddings in places such as Leonard's
of Great Neck or Terrace on the Park.

Oh Taylor, you were the sing-along
at many an engagement party,
you slowed a lot of us down,
you made a lot of mascara run,
and tonight as your voice careens
through the air, there's not a box
of Kleenex anywhere.

Iowa Landscape

Leave the blinds open so I can click on
the Internet photographs of alluvial rain—
as the Biblically swelling plains swallow days
four to six without more than three hours sleep.

T. reminds me we need these preludes:
and there's probably no second life
of the virtual kind (we haven't made love
in months), no hermaphroditic avatar.

He scolds the dog, loudly, harshly,
as it heads for the pond—
a Portuguese Water dog (mine)
in the settlement after fourteen years.

Take nothing else friends advise
otherwise you're braided to the narrative
to the money-mongering lovelessness
driving 146 miles across CT each weekend.

Iowa. Thousands of miles of biofuel
and rising stocks like the tobacco ghosts
of my youth—the rutted smoke shacks
where they dry soy beans? Consider

the effulgence of these salted pills,
the thin shell the jaw clenches and how
tofu raises estrogen levels, sobbing
across Pennsylvania's thick August green

undulating hills and the barely noticeable
anything else that first separation.
Cleveland, five missed exits behind us...
who would ever pay $300 a night

for a Motel 6 in Sandusky? The aspirin's
starting to kick in and the sudden tenderness
of his voice as he cried when I pulled away.
Such an unexpected burst of emotion

catches our throats after a rare morning
of scissored thighs and arms in that impossibly
Chagallesque TV movie where, during rain,
a rabid dog rides an Iowa brown cow in Florida.

Serendi(pity)

Early morning
Breathless rendezvous
At Murray's!

Que quality
Of colander (sieving negativity)

Two minuets for
Angel-haired Liszt

A lifetime
For a couple pages
Of tassel-headed
Deconstructible bliss

In the antholo-eulogy
Considerably cindered

Cinched at the waist

When the goose of
Yuletides shares

Preparation time

*

Last night on the extremes
I got pretty
Goddamned golden

Awakened to the money-taking
& the foul smell of piss
I expel
To try to expel myself

A savaging metaphysical
Awakened in me
In the plaid swatch patterns
Of November Skies

Overpriced paint
Durango Brown

& a vacuum cleaner

For the mother lode of
Anxious 6:30 a.m. traffic-plated
Kabooming

Lips
Sewn shut

To J.—first day of Early Hanukkah
& the only liberal parents left

Who won't visit
With their queer son's friends

Flash of recognition
Counter downed

We get bigger and bigger
On smears
Listed cunningly

Song:

The stick birds patterning

A horde of stitched snowflakes

Tree sans candles

Desert bushes no doubt

Rows of healing men

Hands displayed flatly

To the heavens inverted

Star of David

for my friend J.

Bad Trick

No laws of attraction mandated
By the Supreme Being apply here—
In this tawdry porn-filled leather bar
On the abandoned outskirts of town.

Thursdays the Lick-It Lounge doubles
As queer karaoke but if that tragic
No-butt dude with the over-Botoxed face
Thinks I'm in his league then

Let the evisceration begin, feed
The entrails to the culture vultures,
Pray the rosary beads off their strands.
And how did my own ass sag so soon,

Even in my best butt-cheeky Lucky jeans
And this well-beyond B-list attitude?
Who trolls the bars anymore anyway,
Since the damned Internet? No smoke,

Overpriced drinks, and we all look better
Closer to closing time, jacked on a second
Vodka martini (extra olives please),
Especially after months of expired latex.

But whoa, Mr. vacated-ass can sing,
Fashion casualties aside, and now
Some favorites: "Who's That Girl"
And "Toxic" back to back—"work it"—

I find myself hooting. He winks,
Then follows me into the can
For a little retro-ridiculousness—
Though thankfully those days are over.

He invites me to the Renaissance instead—
A luxury hotel.... I give the friend I came
With the it's-all-wrong-but-I'm-going-anyway-
Sign. We're off miles from my apartment—

Let's hope he doesn't have parasites. Though
He promptly warns he's Republican, fickle,
And now offers to drive me home. Now?
I'd rather jump into this nasty river stink,

Join the floating debris thirty feet
Below, though I'd probably live
And have to walk home wet, and die
Slowly, of pneumonia. If money's

Attracted to me He better show up
Soon! Where's that lanky, love-toy
Lacrosse player I was promised?
I'm next in line at the deli counter.

That's my claim check. And why
Is it that reduced-price day-old
Bread always seems to be in the same
Aisle as the kitty litter? At the Rt. 95

Overpass I'm convinced it would be
Too messy, too much effort to climb
The fifteen-foot safety fence. I'm through
With disfigurement, and body parts.

My mind runs to stabbings, robberies.
None of us is getting any younger. But please
Give back my license and ID. I can't
Wait on a motor vehicle line again. Ever.

Bewitched, Bedraggled, December

Loaded down
On a special broken VCR

Flashes
The not as mean time
at Ipswich

When the light's on
The connection's synapsing

No *langue*
No tongue
Or comfort

What continuum these lips
Are on

To believe in the
Sacredness
Of growing

Red alphabet of wolves

Indifferent room

Disappearance and Modulation

Three broken vertebrae, chronic osteoporosis
  and now memory lapses.... To transition,
naturally I buy a dog: over-determined love
  object, consoler of anticipated grief that will
face the bleak collapse with me each day

as a mother escapes further, each half-developed
  attempt at combating a waning affection;
flailing and floundering, forgetting even how
  to boil greens that help with digestion.
The first stop every visit home, the refrigerator

to examine what's good to eat: instead, head
  protruding, upper compartment ajar, shoulder high,
yes, there's my sweet dog, in the freezer! Swedish
  fish, I call her—a Portuguese Water Dog, I
capitulated to name Marlie, not the same spelling

as the Rastafarian national hero of Jamaica,
  in spite of the sheepdog-length tresses. Marl,
for short, or Marlboro girl, in full camped-up butch—
  aplomb and indignant when folks mistake her
for a poodle...pit bull-poodle mix, I retort!

In this nightmare I've had four times, she's moored
  ice-to-the-touch, almost comatose, no mistaking
her lethargic excitement as she recognizes me—
  fifty-pound frazzle of drool, where the holiday
lamb's usually stored. Mom dons a surgical gown

and matching elbow-length gloves then hushes me
  into a church mouse voice since the dog's resting,
recovering from five-hour, open-heart surgery.
  My mother, dressmaker, seamstress who worked
six days a week, for $492 a month, has proffered

a diagnosis: she hushes me again and reveals forty-six
  expertly sewn stitches and a thirteen-inch lightning
bolt scar on Marlie's tuxedo-patched underside.
  Forty-six, age she was at my birth, medical miracle,
soon enough my own age. And this just in:

a long-term relationship with my partner also
  unraveling. Everything I love is disappearing
permanently frozen in some other emotional strato-
  sphere, all psychic support, inspiration, and Art—
name also of my ex-partner, in this freezer,

in this nightmare, next to the month-old tomato sauce.
  Marlie's "recovering nicely," mother offers
as her surgical gown flaps open behind her back,
  a star-speckled unknowable universe, piercing
in its glittering darkness, a mere arm's length away.

Earthly Possessions (*Errata*)

Can't wake a mile each mourning too weighty for new experience
Can't burn the guitar, urn the sitar at last song
Can't rake away heavenly desertions, approach myself to her eighty

Take the slivered bowls for ice and coleslaw and crab claws
All of the above (she insists) but don't forage for the shot-through, etched
    glasses
The scotch tumblers: fake but yours

& the juice classes, six of each while you're at it, "not too many at once"
She's *vigitant* against the future: about the arithmetic in her left knee
Today's new one: seven ducks of record meat

& the marooned dahlias sucking up to the water—
Inspectors for her hair & she'll have to dig up the bulbs,
Bodega them in the basement, whether the adages

Wash the winnows, melt the wax, more or less

Mise-en-scène

I. *Woman, Car Accident, Sleepless Night*

for L.B. (1966-1997)

We all have opinions
about the reclining woman.

Odalisque in a headband.
Painting or not? Incisors? Eternal refrigerator.

That persistent (hidden) smell
in our kitchen and the traffic:

Crushed collarbone, sternum. Asphyxia.
Just before the end, swerving

when she thought herself spared.

II. *Car Accident, Re-Construction*

a fire every time, car burning
                          '67 Chevy along the road.
How he thrashed about
           in the backseat

              charred box—

just now in the dining room
                  the torchère lamp dims,
the refrigerator's   next room,
          laughter.

        Had we taken out a policy—

this tin taste (sweet potatoes and salsa)—
        the shower beckoning, freshly grouted

stall, the water pounding, naked
and not naked,   house and not house,

a mile from the stranded car
           so much a person

Malevich: Thirty-Four Drawings

almost a palm tree a swirling umbrella drawn with a T-square a
compass a pencil—lead on its side   in 10. bars over rectangular
horizontal slashes that reverberate   shapes disappear   in the
next   they exist   under erasure   a floating cross

everything's framed by looking: a visual pattern a rhythm: a visual
elemental language reconstitutes shapes then disintegrates   nothing
is added in 5.—movements re-form into a ball   an oppressive
unbalanced heavy cross—

an erasable triangle in 9. not clearly edged with penlike injections
from the life-extracting vital syringe: substance-shape-form-color
(ideas of flatness)—then a field with land mines or open infinitesimal
four dimensions of—no snow across this art book naturally flecked
lack of color

14. cousin to the palm-tree umbrellas lightly shaded triangles—
dissipated and reconfigured building echo of the lunar—prototypes
for early Russian cosmonauts: a spotlit vibrant field whose trajectory
is the cosmos the telescope the broken barriers of the reordered lack

of imagery, a disintegration into nothing, parts, antennae that call on
the collective good!

                    Imaginary spaces of Suprematist canvases

for Mayakovsky's verses—covers designed by Rodchenko, rectilinear
and geometric volumes, architecture & grid structures that assert
flatness, not representation! Words are flatnesses/ fragments of
machinery

Montecassino

Relieved
To outlive
A generation of ghosts.
Whistling

Through headstones.
Who'll search
Tobacco Valley
For you, *Mammarella?*

Toward the descending
Necropolis
An old woman
Points the way,

Lantern candles
& directions for sale.
Is that you
In that crypt, beneath

The stairs? Exhumed
Ten years later:
Italy, a small country.
Two-foot

Boxes
Piled high
Fibula bones,
& faces smile

From medallion-shaped
Pendants:
Lovely in black.
Practical.

Zion (Two Sketches)

LET ME CALL MARY GIAIMO

I'm getting too close

To the information

Rimbaud: "I have known all the sons of respectable families."

My deer

Have horns

Not antlers

Cavafy: "My resolution to restrain myself to change, lasted for two weeks
at the very most."

*

IF DANTE BELIEVED IN HELL THEN

Twenty-four days of record

Cold in Utah &

The inversion

Is surely that place

Jan. cold @ the

Professor's house...

A foot of old snow

& that sick feeling

Again rudderless

At the car park

'til three in the morning

"You who taught me

How man makes

Himself eternal"

Pities the sodomites

Writhing in hot sand

In a fiery storm of rain

Harvest

You have untied the tomato plants,
pulled their trivial roots from the ground,

piled the posts holding them,
against the neighbor's fence.

Your gardening shoes conform
to the shape of your feet,

the heels are worn. October—
the moon looms larger

lengthens the shape of the house—
& if I do not disclose his confidences,

I am next to you, not helping really,
I do not know how,

but I will sleep next to you,
nuzzling my fingers

while the neighbor's son steals
into our garden, ravishing it,

littering the yard
kicking up

whatever orphaned history's left.

The Grand Central Clock Will Be Tired Again

With the kids driving home from the District
And the bypass bypassed
The gift I treasure, incidentally, miniatures, *matonies*
That's spangled Italian
Where Abba-esque we will go a-glaring
Later this morning after we've brushed
And met at the station.

So I says to Evelyn
So I says to Chris

Pray: the better part to be more
Interior than the confessional holy water
Made-up thickly for the coffin.

*

Sacred heart

Bleary eyes twitching again
Cantilevered
Between verbs and infinity
This unstitching
Victorian drawl
Manly enchantress

Sacred heart

Who can't appreciate the dancing tongue of the androgynous.
Locks, full red beard, pure olive oil light

No more killing, I say—especially in those
Latest fashionista French cuffs
So what if we wear our shirts open?
Just leave the goddamned pair
Of shoes on & don't take pictures.

Roma Auto

Overture

there where you can see Grottaminarda on rare clear dustless hazeless days and Flumeri—ancient hilltop town above the Area of the Madonna in the Italian air Sturno (stern place) where the river no longer flows before ancient nomadic peoples usurped the resources of Mediterranean cities and dragged primitive autos—oxcarts *buoi* horses stallions of Graecia to Magna Graecia and anachronistically to Turkey to level Troy for more spoils the onslaught of history remedies not the environmental distress

*

Automatic

Roma auto by Fiat only name that comes to me now divorced more and more from this birthplace standard automatic shift—costs more more Euro where a sister's called to settle Cordelia's nothing—to parse the Madonna's land all that's left a five-acre property house-leaky decrepit finally sold they stole the kitchen my parents paid for rightfully theirs kitchens being expensive everywhere—they don't contest the house no contest or interest since they likely misused the earthquake relief money St. Rocco's CCD or St. Anne's of Johnston RI Roma auto near where I write a few miles away all other churches lost to me in abandoned memory cities—

*

Manic

even the toilet seats they stole the fixtures they took from the house that rocked that shook and cracked rightfully yours rightfully theirs up the stairs where the tiles are battered and the rain pours through—that other sister who paid no rent in financial ruin rumors there Rumor a thousand-eyed beast *che bestia é la vecchiaia*—K. beast of burden—stalled auto derelict Roma auto palimpsestic Roma

Terra firma

Asphyxiating and tenanted not fixed or gassed *benzina* Benzocained
and broken auto aught to asphyxiate after two generations this
landed cut from the past Roma auto along the road at the overgrown
field Roma auto the trigger marker maker of bombs—elderly parents
not welcomed in their own home not undeservedly unwelcome these
turning auto wheels of cyclical nostalgia triggered by Fellini in black
and white *Roma* of graveled sputtering soundtrack and rumble empty
tour through the film-abandoned night-lit streets still city my city's
exploded scintillating rubble lights and walls of death notices of the
1980 quake along the road the fallen *Angelo* cousin where my parents
are temporarily living settling their affairs

Angel Copter

now the fallen church the cracked house *lesionata* no liaison the
broke back-house the we-carried-water-from-*sotto-l'angelo*-in-the-
piazza house our first non out-house house IED-ed sharded in the
waking sound dream of language disappearing

Encore

Roma auto automatic without animation *allegro non troppo* slow
motionless and a mother felled and the aria I've been reenacting and
expecting I mouth to mouth her pump her chest to psychic x-ray her
in that order her ardor a door to an immigrant's scars of a language
she no longer perhaps never spoke this lexicon of loss and fish call the
doctor to check the sequence to animate the inanimate the soulless
uncomfortable orphaned one in the end Roma anima never IUD-ed
the pregnancy the birth growth and afterlife the drifting away spread
to the four ends of earth

Auto da fé'

she speaks today in the language of polyglot snorts she repeats herself
repeats—*sporcheggiando* making the language dirty (ironically) by
trying to cage and john it to refine it her Italian *parlando*—her
parlance of staid parlor games of pallor and disbelief when she can no
longer no longer walk place me dead anywhere let me God anywhere
Roma auto I can't hear right from this threshold where they've
forgotten the writing these birthplace words vanishing sounds of the
dozen or so who speak the dialect anymore

*

Anatomical History: Theatre

who'll look for me they'll leave me in some unknown coroner's freeze
case for days—cold there says the animate Roma auto who'll prepare
the vigils don't hate us if we say too much salivate and liquidate if the
words pour a fountain out of Roma auto authority of our own
Jacobean drama authored closer to home (c. 1625) tragedy by
Middleton and my own sister who sues our mother over olives over
olive groves my parents planted painstakingly we live in thickets we
live to love and use and preserve—

*

Redux

her mother's forsaken again destined in old age to go out to Roma
auto as she came in not horse-driven small town loveless hearsed
disappeared olive-less laurel-less to plant and shake and mash and
pest the olives into oil and sell the viscous remains to everyone except
our own gypsy relatives not even dead would she be buried in that
family tomb as if there's another way to go into the tomb—we don't
know Roma auto

Dear Reader: Questions about Sugar

This opal ring, set in gold may be
such a rich good picture to cut out
larger than a real ring, not
the perception of larger:

this icon, now held by a refrigerator magnet
so crisp, the picture floats,
slip finger hole in the imagined
space it creates

like thought, computer-generated
where the boundaries blur, thought
more evanescent than writing
more compressed—an infinitesimally

existent place. There's interference now:
Charlie, my brother-in-law, waking—gently
good morning, Charlie! A walk
down by the bridge with his fiancé

and then questions about sugar—
in the yellow canister in the storeroom,
a wedding...keep looking

Rain Delay

Tied in the eighth inning,
a strikingly bright sky
after a *temporale*, shocking
pink sunburst, then

the slow dissipation, into
don't remember, a fortuitous
flash of personal history.
The best things are ordinary

and out of control at once:
the predictable thunder five
one-one thousands after lightning;
an occasional accolade;

a Rolling Stones concert,
also outdoors, Giants Stadium,
twenty years later than
expected, Mick Jagger as if dubbed

into Japanese. His voice, too,
exploding one thousand feet
per second finally reaching
the bleacher seats

(Upper Tier, Section 320).
Satisfaction.
This far removed?
& fate:

a convenient amnesia,
it didn't happen, it is tragic,
we're all responsible:
our place in the game.

Notes:

"Sri Lanka": besides punning on one of several of Sri Lanka's (colonial) names, this piece also conflates thoughts about identity, the devastating 2004 tsunami and the more recent floods in Sri Lanka, as well as Paul Celan's suicide by drowning in the Seine.

"Built on the Foundation of What Isn't True": references the film *Singing Myself a Lullaby* (2000) directed by Ellen Bromberg, and Douglas Rosenberg. I am grateful to Karen Brennan, beloved professor and friend, for the inspiration of this poem.

"The Weight of Water": "Mortals speak insofar as they listen. They heed the bidding call of the stillness of the dif-ference even when they do not know the call."—Martin Heidegger from "Language." Including this reference to Heidegger in sequence closely after calling Celan to mind, was conceived, among other things, as a meditation on the complex interrelationships and resonances of their work.

"66 Trees": Dario Bellezza, (1944-1996), was a prizewinning Italian poet, novelist, and playwright whose early poetry was championed by Pier Poalo Pasolini, Alberto Moravio, and Elsa Morante. The text referenced here is *Il poeta assassinato* (1996), Bellezza's exposé about Pasolini's murder.

"Broken Kingdom": the film alluded to is *Mr. Blandings Builds his Dream House* (1948), directed by H.C. Potter.

"An Oyster Leads a Dreadful but Exciting Life ...": Swiss avant-garde poet, Blaise Cendrars' cut-ups and his documentary processes, especially in *Kodak*, inspired this piece in which I re-arranged and lightly edited lines from MFK Fisher's *Consider the Oyster* (1941).

"Roma Auto": was conceived as a "sound poem" of sorts and it plays freely with code switching techniques from English to Italian and Italian dialect. When direct translations are not immediately offered, the sound resonances and/or etymological links between words are, I hope, evident enough. I am indebted to Carrie Anne Tocci for the phrase "Cordelia's Nothing" the title of her, as yet, unpublished poetry manuscript.

Acknowledgments:

Special thanks to the editors of the following journals where these poems first appeared or are forthcoming, sometimes in slightly different versions.

2Bridges Review: "Eternal Mercy Hallmark Card," "Iowa Landscape"

American Poetry Review: "66 Trees"

Cimarron Review: "Broken Kingdom"

Colorado Review: "The Weight of Water," "The River"

Connecticut Review: "Theory of Ultimate Willfulness," "Harvest"

Confrontation: "Visit to San Francisco"

Gulf Coast: "More Than a Verb, a Nation"

Interim: "Sri Lanka," from "Zion (Two Sketches)": "If Dante Believed In Hell Then," "Let Me Call Mary Giaimo"

Italian Americana: "Montecassino," "I. Woman, Car Accident, Sleepless Night" from "Mise-en-scène"

Kestrel (Twenty-fifth Anniversary Issue): "Chelsea Apartments Emptying"

LIT: "No Jobs at the Fiat Plant"

Lo-Ball: "'Such a Drag to Want Something Sometime'"

Phati'tude Literary Magazine: "Built on the Foundation of What Isn't True"

Roger: An Art and Literary Magazine: "Millennial Wyoming in Unpopular Imagination, with Codeine"

Shaking Like a Mountain (online): "'Tell it To My Heart,'" "'Such a Drag to Want Something Sometime'"

Shampoo (online): "Bad Trick"

spork: "Home Movies"

Quarterly West: "'Her Eyes Flew Open,'" "Earthly Possessions (*Errata*)"

Yale Review: "Disappearance and Modulation"

"Tell it to My Heart," also appeared in *My Diva*, from the University of Wisconsin Press, 2009; "Rain Delay" in the 2009 *Alhambra Poetry Calendar*, Alhambra Publishing, Betrem, Belgium 2009.

Special thanks especially to Bill Olsen, Marianne Swierenga, Kim Kolbe, and Elizabyth Hiscox for their belief and nurturance, and for making this book a reality. For believing in me and making my work worthwhile, I would like to extend gratitude also to the administration, colleagues, and students at the University of Rhode Island, especially Mary Cappello, Jean Walton, and Martha Rojas.

The University of Rhode Island's Council for Research, and the Hope and Heritage Fund provided much needed financial assistance while working on these poems, as did the PEN/American Osterweil Award, the Kaplen Foundation, and the Provincetown Work Center.

Many dear and accomplished poets and friends have offered editorial suggestions and unflagging encouragement along the arduous journey of this book, especially Edvige Giunta, Donald Revell, Jacqueline Osherow, Hollis Kurman, Mary Giaimo, Talvikki Ansel, Patricia Spears Jones, Tim Cavanaugh, Jerry Williams, Tina Chang, Richard Blanco, Alvin Owens, Kevin McLellan, Tim Liu, Richard Hoffman, Melissa Hotchkiss, Scott Hightower, and Derek Pollard. Thank you all from the deepest parts of me.

photo by Hollis Kurman

Poet, translator, and editor Peter Covino is Associate Professor of English and Creative Writing at the University of Rhode Island. He is the winner of the 2007 PEN American/Osterweil Award for emerging poets and also the author of *Cut Off the Ears of Winter* (New Issues, 2005) and the chapbook *Straight Boyfriend* (2001), winner of the Frank O'Hara Poetry Prize. His co-edited volume, *Essays on Italian American Literature and Culture* recently appeared from Bordighera Press, CUNY (2012).

The Green Rose Prize

2011:   Corey Marks
        The Radio Tree

2010:   Seth Abramson
        Northerners

2009:   Malinda Markham
        Having Cut the Sparrow's Heart

2008:   Patty Seyburn
        Hilarity

2007:   Jon Pineda
        The Translator's Diary

2006:   Noah Eli Gordon
        A Fiddle Pulled from the Throat of a Sparrow

2005:   Joan Houlihan
        The Mending Worm

2004:   Hugh Seidman
        Somebody Stand Up and Sing

2003:   Christine Hume
        Alaskaphrenia
        Gretchen Mattox
        Buddha Box

2002:   Christopher Bursk
        Ovid at Fifteen

2001:   Ruth Ellen Kocher
        When the Moon Knows You're Wandering

2000:   Martha Rhodes
        Perfect Disappearance